The Journey

Joanna King

Copyright © 2015 by Jo Gale

All rights reserved.

No part of this publication may be reproduced, distributed, or transmitted in any form or by any means, including photocopying, recording, or other electronic or mechanical methods, without the prior written permission of the publisher, except in the case of brief quotations embodied in critical reviews and certain other noncommercial uses permitted by copyright law.

Wholesale discounts for book orders are available through Ingram Distributors.

ISBN
978-1-987985-70-2 (paperback)
978-1-987985-69-6 (ebook)

Published in Canada.

First Edition

Table of Contents

A note from the author 1
The Journey 5
The Face 11
Brave 17
Dreamer 19
Summer Love 21
Only Love Knows 25
To Me 29
Evermore 31
Wallflower 35
Morning 37
Waiting 39
Without You 43
Even Now 45
Endless 47
Cycles 51
A Day of Tears 55
When 57
Lost Love 61
Dare 65
Don't 67
The Voice 69
Miss Understood 75
For You 77

Captive	81
Strong	87
You	95
Dad	99
Heal	101
Disappearing	105
Our Love	111
Better Days	115
Nightbird	117
Identity	121
The Stone	127
Oh My Love	129
Watching	131
Seat 22A	135
Letting Go	139
Rite	141
The First Day	145
The Haunted	151
The secret	155
The Last Goodbye	159
Best Friends	165
The Fifth Day	169
The Angel	175
April	181
Journeys End	185

A note from the author

Here is a collection of my poetry in which I have attempted to capture the many moments that occur within a lifetime. Some of these poems have been inspired by my own personal journey, and some have been inspired by the journey of others. My hope is that these poems will encourage and inspire you, and connect with you in some way. You may even find your own journey has been captured within these pages. If you do, know that you are not alone, many others have shared your experiences. Remember it is not about the destination. I hope you enjoy

The Journey.

Joanna King

Thank you to everyone who believed in me. Your words of encouragement helped inspire me to believe in myself.

The Journey

I am leaving my old life
So I can start again anew.
I walk away because I know
Those old roads lead to you.

No good can come from staying,
You will only keep me down.
I'll leave behind all those I know,
And be free of this town.

Though bones in cupboards rattle,

I'm the one who holds the key.

I was never meant to stay here,

It is time that I was free.

I will not give a second glance,

It's time to jump this track.

It's time to break away from bonds,

That crush my soul and back.

I hear my future calling,

It is screaming out my name.

I wasn't meant to live this life,

And I can't stay the same.

Do you feel disconnected?

Like you never have fit in.

That you were meant for more than this,

And *they* are not your kin.

Do you feel there is something,

That you were meant to do?

And all this stuff is wasting time,

There's more than that to you.

They say life is a journey,

And you know what? They are right.

You have to give yourself a chance,

Because you're worth the fight.

Believe you have the courage.

Take heart you're not alone.

Those twists and turns within your life,

Weren't meant to set the tone.

If you can hear my message,

If this can touch your soul,

Know that *you* can reach your dreams,

And you *can* make you whole.

It won't all be plain sailing,

Obstacles will block your way.

But hold on tight to who you are,

You *will* see light of day.

I hope this gives you courage,

These words of mine you hear.

Because we all deserve a life

To treasure and hold dear.

The Face

I went out on my evening walk,
As I was apt to do,
And passed an old forgotten house,
No longer loved or new.

My mind was rambling as it can,
Just idly filling time.
I saw a moon hung high above,
I heard a church clock chime.

When I had almost passed the house,
I turned, and saw you there.
A tiny little face that watched,
And caught me in its stare.

Surprised to find you watching,
Not thinking it was true,
I dared not blink for fear that I
Would lose that sight of you.

I stopped and faced that window.
I think I held my breath.
Transfixed to find that tiny face,
So held 'tween life and death.

A young child's face stared longing,

    Trapped past the window pane.

How long it waited, I knew not,

    Nor what it hoped to gain.

And yet we watched each other,

    As questions filled my head.

How long had you been waiting?

How long had you been dead?

Time passed, but had no meaning.

I was spellbound in your stare.

So small and unassuming,

    So totally aware.

I did not dare to turn away,

But then I watched you fade,

And staring at that empty place,

I wished that you had stayed.

Alone once more that evening,

I ventured on my way.

My thoughts were filled with you of course,

As they would every day.

Could I unleash the mystery?

Could I unfold your tale?

I hoped to find out all I could,

I hoped I would not fail.

A child's face in the window,

Watching, wishing to be free.

Waiting, as I took my walk,

Watching out for me.

A photograph in archives,

A child lost by the flame.

A cruel death on that winters night,

Another soul to claim.

But still you wait here watching,

When you should have left this place.

I know that I shall not forget,

That pale and lonely face.

BRAVE

I know that you can do this,

It is not beyond your reach.

Though it takes tremendous courage,

There are lessons you must teach.

You will overcome this moment,

You will see the other side.

You will do this without failing,

You will take it in your stride.

Do not listen to those voices,

They just make you scared and weak.

They are not there to help you,

They are there to keep you meek.

You can lean on me if it helps you.

Let my whispers fill your ears.

You're brave and naught can stop you,

Believe this all your years.

Dreamer

The whisperings of evening,
The silver light of moon,
Those misty hazy memories,
Of a never ending tune.

The scent of perfumed flowers,
The twinkling stars above,
Just you and I together,
Wrapped in folds of love.

The sounds of laughter drifting,

The picture coming clear.

The loneliness of waking,

To find I dreamt you here.

I dream of you whilst waiting,

Imagining the kiss.

I wait for you to find me,

And take me from all this.

Wait- once again it's evening,

And look, I see us dance.

Can you see the same dream?

Or will we meet by chance?

Summer Love

I opened up the window,
'Twas the kind of night I like.
I listened as the rain fell,
And watched the lightening strike.

The trees outside were swaying,
I could hear their restless cry.
Up above the thunder roared,
The noise fled through the sky.

My mind began to wander,
It was filled with thoughts of you.
Lazy, hazy summer days,
A bright and dazzling hue.

A picnic in the country,
Cheap champagne to quench our thirst.
Hoping I was all you'd want,
You were my last and first.

Those sweet remembered kisses,
Burning hotter than the sun.
Locked in such a sweet embrace,
We laughed out loud in fun.

Your smile was warm and tender,
How I hoped that you would stay.
And I could keep believing,
You'd always be this way.

A glimpse of love I'd cling to,
That glimpse was all I'd know.
Your love was for the summer,
You knew that you would go.

I thought we were forever,
And I gave you all I had.
I told you that I loved you,
I thought it made you glad.

Now staring out the window,

Listening to that raging storm,

A new love stirring needs me,

A new love keeps me warm.

I turn and leave that fury.

All that chaos running wild,

And gently stroke the sleeping face,

Of my beloved child.

Only Love Knows

I've seen love, oh so many times,
Like a late night picture show.
I've seen love passing quickly,
And I've seen love growing slow.

I've seen love look at all my friends,
I've seen love look at me.
I've seen love wash away my tears,
And change the things I see.

Love spreads its arms around you,

Its warmth invades your heart.

I've felt love take away my breath,

And feared to let it start.

I've seen love, oh so many times,

I've seen love come and go.

But I never seem to understand,

And I guess I'll never know.

Why love is often lonely,

Why it always brings me pain.

It can be like morning sunshine,

But it feels like evening rain.

Perhaps I've seen too many times,

That love lies in my dreams.

And though I thought I knew it,

Only love knows what it means.

To Me

To me love is in freedom,

That can't tie me to your side.

Love is the joy of knowing,

That there's just no need to hide.

To me love is in whispers,

That float on passing cloud.

Love is the single feathered bird,

That leaves the madding crowd.

To me love is the morning,

When the dew glistens like snow.

Love is the sound of silence,

Which has nowhere else to go.

To me love is in sweet dreams,

That can keep me satisfied.

Love is the shimmer of the moon,

Because the sun has died.

To me love is in living,

In these moments full of peace.

Love is this lonely dreaming,

That I guess will never cease.

Evermore

I love these treasured moments,

When I sit alone with you.

When life can't interrupt us,

There's nothing it can do.

Protected in our haven,

You are peaceful in my touch.

I only want to hold you,

I want that very much.

I cannot hear your breathing,

Though I know you wait with me.

We move as one, united,

It's like it's meant to be.

We're bound to one another,

I just close my eyes and smile.

Knowing one day soon you'll come,

And stay with me a while.

I wonder what you'll look like.

Will you have my curly hair?

Are you listening to my voice?

To know me anywhere?

You are my darling baby,

You're the child I'm waiting for.

I promise to protect you,

And love you evermore.

Wallflower

Is that you standing there my wallflower?
Are you hiding whilst stood in plain view?
Do you think if you hold your breath just a bit more,
That no one here will notice you?

Are you watching the people here quietly?
Taking everything in that they do.
Have you ever once wanted to run from the wall?
Have you ever once just wanted to?

You hide, and yet sometimes I see you,

I saw you once reach out your hand.

I have seen you stand still, with the hope in your eyes,

As they smile at the place where you stand.

But they will not see you wallflower.

They see only the brash and the loud.

Your loneliness fills you, and pours from your face

As you stand in this room with this crowd.

Morning

The sun is slowly rising,
As I watch the birth of day.
The clouds are gently forming,
As the night goes on its way.

The birds are busy chatting,
Pretty songs surround the air.
Soundless wings are flapping,
As they fly to anywhere.

Sweet smells fill my nostrils,
Aromas full of spring.
The scents of countless flowers,
Speak the messages they bring.

The bees are busy working,
Too intent on work to spy,
The figure at the window,
Who watches as they fly.

The feeling in the morning,
That I do not know it all,
That there is something greater,
Leaves me feeling very small.

Waiting

I sit here at the window,

Where I sit each passing year.

Surrounded by my memories,

Of all that I hold dear.

The scenes outside keep changing,

As seasons come and go.

Cocooned inside I wait here,

As I watch it ebb and flow.

I don't know why I linger,

I feel my life is done.

I sit here at the window,

As I watch another sun.

Don't worry, I'm not eager,

I will run the course of time.

But somehow it seems pointless,

I am so long past my prime.

I've seen countless springs and summers,

I've seen falls and winters too.

But I am growing weary,

There seems nothing left to do.

Why do I sit here waiting?

What on earth do I wait for?

I do not belong in your world,

I don't want to anymore.

So if sometime you see me,

Quietly sitting all alone.

An old forgotten soul who doesn't

Hear the telephone.

Wonder what my name is.

Wonder what my life has been.

For I was standing where you are,

When I was once a teen.

Without You

Without you in my life,

To hold my hand when I am low,

Would mean a life so empty,

There'd be nowhere left to go.

Without you here beside me,

Giving strength when I am weak,

Would mean no point in looking,

For the answers that I seek.

Without your love around me,

When my bleakest moods take hold,

Would mean no point in living,

Just no point in growing old.

Without you, oh without you,

All this would be too much,

I need your light, your strength, your love;

I need your guiding touch.

Even Now

Sometimes I'm caught quite unaware,
And find myself in vacant stare.
A simple gesture, simple word,
Can fill my mind with sounds unheard.

Though many days have passed since then,
I'm taken back to that time when,
I felt my lips against your skin,
So cold because you were not in.

I have my days so black with pain,

It seems there's nothing left to gain.

I miss you so, you can't know how,

Time has no meaning, even now.

Endless

No one has ever made me feel,

The way you seem to do.

I hang on every word you say,

And love to look at you.

Butterflies fly freely,

As my stomach starts to churn.

Anticipation rises,

As I soon begin to burn.

Staring at your mouth,

I am imagining your kiss.

Hoping that you want

To take me far from all of this.

Could we somewhere secret find?

A place where we could hide.

Where we could open up our hearts,

And leave them open wide.

I close my eyes and suddenly,

I see us hand in hand.

You smile because you found me,

And now you understand.

You gently move the strand of hair
That falls across my face,
And gaze into my eyes
As I'm transported from this place.

Then slowly moving closer,
I am lost beyond my will.
And it takes every strength I have
To keep on standing still.

I hear you speak my name,
And I am overwhelmed with joy.
It sounds so gentle from your lips,
And leaves me feeling coy.

I had thought once that love

Was something I would never feel.

Not meant to be part of my life,

I tried to keep it real.

Yet here you stand before me,

As I melt under your gaze.

I know from here on there will be

More endless loving days.

Cycles

I've known loneliness in my life.
I've felt emptiness and pain.
Perhaps you would not think it,
If you looked at me again.

I know that place you're hiding.
Dragged myself up from the dirt.
I learned to cover up the marks,
The darkness and the hurt.

We're all the walking injured.

All hiding scars which show,

That no one lives this life unmarked,

It's not the way to grow.

But sometimes darkness finds you,

When you never meant to fall.

It creeps and clings and smothers,

It is answering your call.

When bad things happen to you,

Know that these things too shall pass.

It won't all stay so bleak and grim,

Or stay an empty glass.

You were not meant to go there,

It is not meant that you stay.

Hang on, and you will see the tide

Is turning day by day.

Take heart and find the courage,

The toll bell has not rang.

Life moves us all in cycles,

On the path of Yin and Yang.

A Day of Tears

I knew that when I saw you one last time

There would be pain.

Knowing there would be no more

And nothing left to gain.

But when we said our last goodbye,

I smiled and watched you leave.

Hoping you would not forget,

And I could learn to grieve.

That day was always coming,

You were ready, that was true.

I watched you spread your wings and fly,

I watched the joy of you.

You are where I know you should be,

You are who you're meant to be.

But leaving you behind

Was very near the death of me.

I could not cry back there,

I could not let you see my tears.

I know there will be many more,

Throughout these passing years.

But life goes on as ere it must,

And I have played my part.

I am not your ending,

I am only just the start.

When

When darkness falls upon you,

And straws are all you clutch.

When life is for the taking,

Beyond the loving touch.

When happy times remembered,

Bring tears that fill your eyes.

And bitter words repeated,

Are the love before it dies.

When days you fill are empty,

Not worth a second look.

And words heard have no meanings,

But those you have mistook.

When sweet words bring back memories,

Of days both dead and gone,

Don't get to thinking that it isn't

Worth the struggle on

When life won't give you answers,

But just laughs behind your back,

And people won't believe

It's just the confidence you lack.

If loneliness surrounds you,

Pushing lovers far away,

Until they are but dreams

You can recall another day.

Don't think your life is useless,

Meant to stay that way for good.

Don't think you can't be loved

Because, they never understood.

Don't blind yourself with pity,

For then you'll never know,

Surviving isn't living,

And love, those feelings grow.

Lost Love

What was I thinking? I don't know,
I never should have let you go.
I thought you'd always keep me warm,
And give me shelter from the storm.

I never thought that we would end,
You were my lover and my friend.
I thought that we were meant to be,
And you would always walk with me.

I took for granted all you gave,

And I'll regret that to my grave.

If I had said I loved you more,

Would you have sought that open door?

I made mistakes, more than a few,

The greatest one was losing you.

I shall regret, I was a fool,

And cool hearts aren't so very cool.

But you've moved on, and I must too,

I never thought it's what you'd do.

I know that phone will never ring,

And sad songs are the ones I'll sing.

An emptiness I'd thought was gone,

Has filled me now we two are one.

A love now lost, a love now past,

Grips me in its shadow fast.

If we by chance should meet again,

I'll hope that you too feel this pain.

That you'll regret you did not stay,

And that you let *me* get away.

Dare

Are you out there looking,

Searching every face you see?

Do you know you're biding time,

Whilst trying to find me?

Should I search for you?

Dare I dream that you are there?

For so long now it seems,

I have not even seemed to care.

Do you dream of when we'll meet?
Do you hope it will be soon?
Are you heavily in thought,
As we both stare up at the moon?
Do you wonder where I am?
Do you wonder at my voice?
For if we by chance meet,
We shall not either have a choice.

Dare I think of you at all?
Dare I hope that you will come?
Should I wonder what you look like?
Or where you have come from?
Dare I dream of gentle hands,
And love that's bold and true?
Dare I allow myself
To even dare to dream of you?

Don't

Don't waste your tears on a love

That doesn't grow.

Don't waste your feelings on

A man who doesn't know.

Don't cry alone when your

Picturing his face.

Broken hearts fall easily

But never leave a trace.

The Voice

Do you have a voice inside,

That lets you know you can't be free?

Do you hear it sometimes screaming,

Or whispering "It's me".

Do you have a voice inside you,

Condescending you in shame?

Letting you know *you*'re the one,

You're the one to blame.

Do you hear it laughing at you?

Poking at you with each word.

Tearing you apart because

It's all you've ever heard.

Do you have a voice inside,

That keeps you locked, and chained, and beat?

Keeping your head down,

As you stare lamely at your feet.

Do you hear it in the silence?

Can you hear it in the crowd?

Never going very far,

And always talking loud.

Do you have a voice inside?

That voice who says it's you.

As you pretend faked ignorance,

That you *are* strong, and true.

That little voice that's burrowed deep,

So deep inside of you.

Have you shaken your fist at it?

Have you screamed 'til you are blue?

Have you found that it is laughing,

As it makes a fool of you?

That little voice inside you,

Seems to hold some special key,

And fights for its survival,

It is used to being free.

It loves to haunt your dreams at night,

It loves to hold you near.

It says it shares itself with you,

You've nothing else to fear.

I can't tell you not to listen,

Though you know deep down its true.

I won't tell you it's ridiculous,

There's more than this in you.

I can tell you every cliché,

I can reason with your mind.

I know that you'll agree

Because there's more than pain you'll find.

No matter how the years pass,

That voice will never age,

And one day you will find

Your body too is now a cage.

Will you really let it take you?

Keep you down each wasted day.

Or will you save yourself from that,

And push it far away?

I hope you find the courage,

No one else believes its lies.

You are much more than you believe,

And you *can* cut the ties.

That voice you've always hated,

That voice not even yours,

Snuff it out, and turn it off,

Shake off its sharpened claws.

I can be the new voice.

The voice that says, "You can"

The voice that says you stand a chance,

Embrace your fellow man.

I know you have it in you,

You are much more than you know.

Believe in me, as I do you,

There's nowhere you can't go.

So lick your wounds, and dry your eyes,

And hold your head up high.

Take a chance, and learn to live,

Begin anew like I.

Miss Understood

Because you hate to help me,

In any shape or form,

I learned to do things by myself,

'Til it became the norm.

I will not ask what you think,

For you will think I'm weak.

Behind my back your words of lies,

Are words I will not speak.

I'm not sure how it happened,

I see it brings you joy.

Your whispered words that are not true,

Your cunning, sneaking ploy.

Condemned for being stronger,

An island I became.

Surrounded by a sea of hurt,

Within a sea of shame.

Forever looking onwards,

I am longing to be free.

Where I can truly be myself,

And you see only me.

For You

If you've felt that your life

Just isn't worth the pain.

That sadness overwhelms you,

Soaking you like falling rain.

Your heavy heart is slowing,

You are praying it will stop.

The blood flow through your veins

Just isn't worth a single drop.

If you are tired of trying,

And your soul just craves to sleep.

You do not wish to stay here,

There is nothing left to keep.

There's no more tears to cry,

You are a desert in the sun.

You do not look for help because

You never learned to run.

Do not give up on yourself.

I hope to help you see,

That inside everyone is pain,

There's pain inside of me.

If you can drag yourself up,

The binds that keep you there,

Will fall and break upon the ground,

For this shall be my prayer.

It hurts to see you hurting.
You are not alone my friend.
If you can just take courage from
The message that I send.
You are worth more than you think,
They're not worth a second chance.
If they have left you crippled,
I will help to make you dance.

I'll help you see a new world,
And those blinkers will be gone.
You never really lived before,
There's battles to be won.
Please hear these words I'm saying,
They're for you and you alone.
Try opening your heart,
You know it isn't made of stone.

Captive

I took every day for granted,

Treated every day the same.

Thought everything would always be,

Like every day that came.

But change, it was a coming,

Though it hid beyond my sight.

It came and stole the life I knew,

It took away my fight.

I learned fast to adapt,

But not without a price to pay.

I learned to hide within myself,

I learned what not to say.

A body can be broken,

A will can snap in two.

But hearts can mend, and heal, and grow,

Yours beats inside for you.

Resigned to my new fate,

I was a shell without a hope.

I didn't dare to dream or pray,

For more than I could cope.

I just survived for livings sake,

-I had no need to live,

My destiny in others hands,

With nothing left to give.

Freedom is a word,

That holds no meaning to the free.

A precious thing, which can be lost,

As it was lost to me.

There is not always need for chains,

For chains aren't always seen,

And yet they bind, and trap, and snare,

It's as it's always been.

In darkest times I begged for peace,

An end to all the pain.

It never came, and so I learned

To mimic life again.

It's hard when you are drowning,

To see people watch you drown.

And never show a helping hand,

But smile without a frown.

If I were standing in their shoes,

Would I act in that way?

Would I pretend to never see,

And be content to stay?

I want to think I'm not the same,

My voice would right a wrong.

But now I think I do not know—

I don't think I'm that strong.

When all you've ever known

Is taken by a stronger hand.

When you are bruised and broken,

And still fail to understand.

You are your only hope,

For no one cares how far you fall.

No one will risk their life for yours,

No one will risk it all.

I say to all you lucky ones,

Who never gave a thought,

Appreciate all that you have,

And all you have been taught.

Be kind to one another,

Help each other all you can,

For there- but by the grace of God

Go you my fellow man.

STRONG

I never wanted to be strong,

I didn't want to know I couldn't break.

Didn't need to find my back-bone,

Didn't feel the need

To watch you bleed,

But I couldn't let you take.

You said you loved us,

Was it true?

Could you twist that knife if so?

Could you cause such pain

And never care?

The answer's Yes, I know.

Love is not what you believe,

I see it now so clear.

You live an empty soulless life,

And we don't want you near.

Even now it seems you lie,

And sadly every breath you steal,

Is wasted on an empty life,

That never cared to feel.

You play the game a victim,
As you blind all those you tell.
You wallow in their pity,
On your lonely road to Hell.

You know nothing of compassion.
Mercy, doesn't mean a thing.
Love, is just an empty word,
The gold band just a ring.

Your heart is black and empty.
Your soul is lost and weak.
You only listen to *your* thoughts,
Your ears can't hear *us* speak.

I do not understand you,

You have changed each passing year.

You are someone I don't care to know,

You kill all we hold dear.

So wrapped up in yourself,

There was no room for us to breathe.

You cared for no one else it seemed,

We simply had to leave.

Your ego tried to hurt us.

Did its best to maim and kill.

We hid, and ran for cover,

We are hiding from you still.

You care not for our children,
They were pawns for you to play.
Their thoughts and feelings didn't count,
You thought they'd always stay.

You didn't think we'd leave you,
Always thought you held the key.
You never thought we'd find the strength,
That strength, it came from me.

I will not let you hurt us.
I will not let you win.
I'll fight you on my deathbed.
I will never once give in.

Our childrens lives are happy.
Though you'll never know, its true.
They have dreams, and goals... ambitions,
They still have no need of you.

You hoped we'd fail without you.
You hoped we'd want you back.
You wanted us to lose our way,
Fall from the beaten track.

But whose life reeks of pity?
Whose empty life is dead?
Who blames the world for every fault?
Who hangs on by a thread?

I don't feel sorry for you.
We all reap that which we sow.
Our lives are rich in love and deed,
We continue thus to grow.

Perhaps one day you'll realize,
Maybe one day you will see,
That all the pain you caused us,
Just helped us to be free.

I do not think you'll recognize,
That what you did was wrong.
I think you'll die believing,
I was evil all along.

But I never wanted to be strong.

I didn't want to know I couldn't break.

Didn't need to find my backbone.

Didn't feel the need

To watch you bleed,

But I couldn't let you take.

You

The sky is dark grey,

But what do you care,

Dark clouds are looming,

There's a chill in the air.

Thunder is rolling,

The wind tries to howl,

Bitterness creeps,

It is out on the prowl.

An iciness hides,

As it grasps at your breath,

And a fear starts to build,

As you recognize death.

It stares back unblinking,

You try to hold still.

It is silently patient,

And nips at your will.

Though all is thought lost,

Deep inside burns a flame,

That will never extinguish,

It has carved out your name.

It will burn throughout conflict,

It will burn beyond tears.

It will shine like a beacon,

And guide all your years.

You are strong without knowing,

When you thought you were weak.

You have found without looking,

And know not what you seek.

Do not doubt in the darkness,

Do not tremble in fear.

You are more than you think,

You are everything dear.

Yes those dark clouds are looming,

As they threaten to fall.

And the rain starts to splatter,

It has answered the call.

But ahead lies the sunshine,

Ahead lies the light,

As nature responds in a deafening sight.

You can never give up,

You can never give in.

You are all that you need,

You are destined to win.

Hear the voice deep inside,

It protects you alone,

As you walk down that path,

Built on mortar and stone.

In those times when you question,

Do not doubt what I know,

You are loved, you are precious,

And you helped me to grow.

Dad

When you first saw my face did it move you?
Were you filled up with joy at the sight?
Did you wonder how far life would take me?
Did you tuck me up safe every night?

Did you pick me up each time I fell down?
Did you help me from losing my way?
Did you watch me with pride fit for bursting?
Did you secretly wish I would stay?

Then why did you never once tell me?

Why not show all the love we could share?

Why keep it all locked up inside you?

Or was it just simply not there?

For now it is too late to tell me....

Now words cannot ever be said,

And all of those things you did badly,

Will always remain in my head.

I wish I could mourn at your passing,

I wish I could cry tears of pain.

Instead I feel nothing inside me,

My feelings for you were in vain.

Heal

You think you are the only one
To feel that pain you feel.
But you must know that everyone
Has known that pain is real.

Those tears that fall down from your face
Hurt you with every drop,
And watching you I only want
That pain you feel to stop.

You did not think it possible

To hurt inside so deep.

You search for answers as you close

Your eyes to hide in sleep.

It's fact that sometimes in your life

Things just won't go to plan.

But don't think you can just give up,

We all do what we can.

You'll love again you know it,

Though right now you can't see,

That love that you were chasing

Simply wasn't meant to be.

Just give yourself a little time,

And in that time you'll mend.

Then you will find your way back here,

For this is not the end.

Disappearing

I know who I am,
I have always known that face.
I know the street I live in,
I know this is my place.

I know who I am,
These hands of mine are strong.
They've built the life in which I live.
The life where I belong.

I know who I am,

But lately I am not so clear.

I feel unsure of many things,

I feel unspoken fear.

I know who I am,

But at times I am unaware.

I just stop what I'm doing,

And wonder what I'm doing there.

I know who I am,

But I do not know my name.

At first it seemed a joke of sorts.

But this is not a game.

I know who I am,

I know I should know who you are.

I wish I could hold on but,

I have drifted on too far.

I know who I am,

I am the one you cannot see.

I've disappeared inside myself,

And now you can't find me.

I don't know who I am,

I don't know where I've been, or why,

I don't know what it is you want,

I don't know why you cry.

I don't know who I am,

I am now lost along the way.

I used to be somebody,

Back in my yesterday.

I know who you are,

I know who you used to be.

I watched you slowly fade away,

And disappear from me.

I know who you are,

But now I know you won't be back.

And all I have are memories,

The memories you lack.

I know who you are,

I know that face so well.

But you left quite some time ago,

And just forgot to tell.

I know who you are,

I will stay until you die.

You are the one I'll always love,

You are the reason why.

I know who you are,

You are more than this, and fear.

I'm watching as you fade away,

And slowly disappear.

Our Love

I have tried to understand you,

When I don't know what you mean.

I have tried to tell you that my love

Is real, and not a dream.

I have tried to give you loving,

When I gaze into your eyes,

And the words of tenderness I speak

Are true, and not my lies.

I have tried to show you feelings,
That are growing in my heart.
And the love I want to show you
Wants to think we'll never part.
But you are always out of reach,
And I can't seem to cope.
And the love I want to show you,
Is a dream that lives in hope.

I have tried to show you clearly,
That this love of mine is real.
And if you opened up your heart
You'd know just how I feel.
I have tried to wait so patiently
But time is dragging on,
And when I turn to speak to you
I find that you have gone.

Why is it that you never want
To know what's in my head?
For if you keep on playing games
I'll wish that I were dead.
I've tried for so long now,
It seems I'm almost giving up.
And I guess it's just a dream,
And we won't share the wedding cup.

How foolish love can make us,
No, I'll never love again.
I'll turn a blind eye to you
And to all the other men.
If you had only seen the love
I tried so hard to show,
I wouldn't be here crying
For a love we'll never know.

Better Days

When cold winds freely blow on lands,
And fingers reach from trees,
When barren soil weeps, and suffers
From its allergies.

When hearts like empty vessels fall,
And love is but a word.
Are lonely days remembering
The sounds they never heard?

When silver linings fade from view,

And strangled grey clouds hang.

When empty hedgerows line the fields

Where birds have never sang.

When life is always winter,

And trees are always bare,

Does nature cry remembering

When better days were there?

Nightbird

I listen for the Nightbird,

As it marks the end of day.

I can forget my worries,

And words I longed to say.

I'm waiting for the Nightbird,

It is turning in the sky.

The sunset lights reflections,

As I listen for its cry.

I long to touch the Nightbird,

Feel its feathers in my hand.

But know that in a moment,

It can leave me where I stand.

Hear soft wings of the Nightbird,

Moving gently in the air.

The strength that lies in flying,

Has me longing to be there.

I have never seen the Nightbird,

I have only heard its sound.

It speaks of captured comfort,

To those who are Earth bound.

The Nightbird starts the journey,

To the bright side of the Earth.

It starts the shadows moving,

As the night begins its birth.

The quietness of the Nightbird,

Sings a song that's strong and deep.

It tells me to surrender,

As it helps me fall asleep.

I have never heard the Nightbird,

When it leaves my mind and soul.

It changes lands of brightness,

To land's as black as coal.

Oh but I love the Nightbird,

With its promises of peace.

Securities of knowing,

That its journey will not cease.

So fly to me my Nightbird,

Let your wings caress my face.

And help me to erase those things,

That dreams want to replace.

Identity

When I was young I used to wonder
What my life would be.
I had my name, I had my home,
I had my family.
Not set upon a straight course,
Not knowing what I'd do,
I just meandered down a path,
In hopes that I'd find you.

Too soon the time to venture came,

And so I left that school.

Forced into a world,

But no exception to the rule.

Too old for education,

Too young to trust the plan,

Searching for you nightly,

In the face of every man.

And when I thought I'd found you,

How I let you win my heart.

I did all they expected,

Thinking this would be the start.

I gave myself completely,

Thinking you would do the same.

I never thought that you would play,

A deeper, darker game.

Somehow the years passed by,
And children filled my world with joy.
I thought they'd make a difference,
That loving girl and boy.
They only altered *my* heart,
They only changed *my* fate,
As slowly you became a man,
That we would learn to hate.

And when I found the courage,
When I had had my fill,
When I decided that was it,
You would not break my will.
We left not looking back,
We left just clinging to be free,
And I knew not where we would end,
Nor what that end would be.

Alone again after so long,

Not knowing who I was,

I tried to find myself again,

I tried to just because.

Looking for identity,

I felt so lost and sad,

Annoyed to have lost everything,

Just everything I'd had.

But slowly as days passed,

I noticed something in me grow,

A feeling I would be alright,

A confidence I'd know.

I don't know where it came from,

I never thought I'd see,

A strength and independence,

Just flowing out of me.

And now if you should see me,

If you passed by me one day,

You'd never in a million years

Think I'd have much to say.

But if you are in my shoes,

The ones I did not keep,

Remember you *can* change your life,

And not pretend to sleep.

The Stone

The stone fell to the ground,

It had stayed true and found its mark.

It had fulfilled its destiny,

And now lay still and dark.

Who could have thought such power,

Lay hidden in its course?

Who could foresee the strength

That it would wield with such a force?

A tiny little pebble,

Insignificant by sight.

A harbinger of death,

And yet a mystery of light.

Forgotten as it fell,

Not ever sought out where it lay.

What else the final outcome,

If not found that fateful day?

The shepherd came upon it,

Thought to use it in his plan.

A boy who would change history,

And grow to be a man.

A child to kill a giant,

A stone which lies forgot.

A sign of times a changing,

A sign of times begot.

Oh My Love

Oh my love, you'll never know
What pain it took to leave.
I didn't want to go because
I knew my heart would grieve.

Oh my love, the dream has gone
And so I cannot stay.
We both must wake alone at dawn
To face that lonely day.

Oh my love, so gentle that

I could not watch your face.

Because I knew that if I did

I could not leave this place.

Oh my love, remember me

And all those dreams we keep.

Because we are still lovers when

We close our eyes and sleep.

Watching

I followed you today.
I stood behind you on the train.
I smelled the clean scent of your hair,
Your softly tousled mane.

I saw you at your desk.
The endless papers left to sign.
Mechanically you set to work,
And signed each dotted line.

I reached my hand out once.

Thought I would show how much I care.

Hoped it would bring you comfort,

To know I'm here, not there.

I know you didn't feel it.

I couldn't wipe away that tear.

I just stood watching uselessly,

And you had no idea.

You ate your lunch alone.

As sadness wrapped you in its shroud.

It hurt so much to see your pain,

But I am not allowed.

I'm not allowed to help you.

But I do not have to leave.

You do not have to be alone,

Though that's what you believe.

Back home again I watched.

I watched you drink a cup of tea.

I knew what you were thinking,

Your thoughts were filled with me.

And when you went to bed,

I saw you cry yourself to sleep.

You know I would do anything,

For you to never weep.

I never should have left.

But we can't choose the time to go.

We learn our lessons whilst we live,

For this is how we grow.

But I will wait here with you.

There's no hurry, I can stay.

And even though you do not know,

I'm with you every day.

Seat 22A

The landscape keeps on changing,
Though the scene is just the same.
A cargo full of people, but
None of them has a name.

The third hour comes and passes,
I am still left on the track.
It seems to me that there can be
No ever looking back.

Countless cups of coffee,

For a change I'll have some tea.

The wheels, they keep on rolling,

Like those waves ahead of me.

The train picks up its speed,

Until we're swaying in our seat.

Beelzebub's behind us,

It's the clock we have to beat.

The man in front is staring

Eager eyes that watch my chest.

Should I tell him what I think?

Or put it all to rest?

The train is slowing down,
Another station comes in view.
That man it seems is leaving,
With the cloud hung over you.

Hope it won't be too long,
My arms and legs all ache.
And this weariness I'm feeling,
Is a feeling I can't shake.

My journey's just begun,
And yet it feels I'm at the end.
Catch the view which disappears
Before we turn the bend.

But no one takes much notice,

As I leave my seat to go.

Everyone's so busy,

They don't really want to know.

Letting Go

Somebody said that if I have
To beg you please to stay,
Then you should not be in my life,
And you should go away.

If you can't see my yearning,
If you long to be free,
Then I should not be begging you
To please stay here with me.

And if I could be brave I know

That I would say Goodbye,

And I would not be crying,

Or begging to know Why?

But though I know all of these things,

My heart won't care to know,

That you will still be leaving,

And I must let you go.

Rite

When I heard you were coming

I was filled with such surprise,

And thus I felt the same way

As I gazed into your eyes.

I slowly came to know you,

You took away my breath,

And I knew I would love you

Right up until my death.

You changed my life completely.

I was proud to watch you grow.

You altered everything I was,

Changed everything I know.

My life became a different place,

I saw it through your eyes.

I saw the wonder of this world,

And soared uncharted skies.

And slowly as the years passed,

I watched the joy of you.

Loving every moment,

Loving everything you do.

I see you fully grown now yet,

To me you'll always be,

The child I gave my life to,

Gave my life so willingly.

You've filled my life with treasures,

I'm so grateful that you came.

Your eyes betray the love you feel,

We are one and the same.

I hope you feel I always

Gave you everything I could.

Protecting you and guiding you

Just like a Mother should.

Now here we are in my life,

Tables turned, and here you sit,

Watching me with loving eyes,

We both know this is it.

Remembering our first Hello

Won't help this last Goodbye.

I'll leave you as I found you,

With this last contented sigh.

The First Day

"You'll never make new friends
If you don't try," my mother said,
And thus I made my way to school,
Whilst words danced in my head.
A weak smile plastered thickly
On my face began to fade,
As entering the school
I broke the promises I'd made.

The new kid, on the first day,

In a school that didn't care.

Pretending to be friendly,

As a sea of faces stare.

Waiting to be pointed

To the table where I'll sit.

Staring at my feet, because

I know that this is it.

I feel their eyes bore holes,

In all those places on my back.

And try to hide that after all,

It's confidence I lack.

The minutes drag by slowly,

As her words fade in my head.

And thus I sit there meekly,

In a world I've come to dread.

At last the school bell rings,

And thunderous noise propels the room.

And I am forced to leave my desk,

And face upcoming doom.

The lunchroom beckons as I try

To find an empty seat,

Wishing I was somewhere else,

With no one here to meet.

At last a lonely corner,

Catches eyes that fill with tears.

I take my place and realize,

I'm old beyond my years.

The odd one in the bunch,

I am the one that can't fit in.

To all extent and purposes

I take it on the chin.

But deep inside a feeling,
Like I'm drowning takes a hold.
I smile in vain remembering,
The words I have been told.
So tired of endless questions,
'What's your name?' and 'Where you from?'
I do not want to be here,
Someone older made me come.

Does it matter who I am?
I know I can't belong.
Pretending to be someone else,
Just leaves me feeling wrong.
Hating every moment,
Feeling lost in every place.
Loneliness engulfs me,
It is etched upon my face.

Back in class I notice,

Someone warmly holds a stare.

Should I offer up a smile,

To show that I am there?

Plucking up the courage,

I prepare to try once more,

Knowing that if all else fails,

I'll soon be out the door.

A pair of gentle eyes look at me

As I try to breathe.

And once again I'm filled with hope,

Perhaps I will not leave.

A soul who seems to see me,

Who recognizes pain,

Who knows the agony of wanting

To be free again.

The Haunted

I saw you placing flowers

On a grave I did not know.

I watched as you began to cry,

And slowly moved to go.

I followed where you ventured,

Though it seemed you did not see.

Your thoughts were in such turmoil,

That you never noticed me.

Whose graveside did you visit?
For whom do those tears fall?
How could I ever tell you,
It won't matter after all?

They cannot hear you crying,
Only I can see you here.
They left so very long ago,
So long ago my dear.

You're caught within this moment,
Unaware that you are dead.
Thinking that you are the one
Who's grieving here instead.

I do not mean to scare you,

I don't want you to fret,

I only wish our paths had crossed,

And when we'd lived we'd met.

It's too late now for wishing,

There are things that cannot be.

And though you do not know it,

You are haunted here with me.

The secret

You think I do not know

That *I'm* the one you want to see.

You think this, for you know,

That I'm aware you are not free.

Your eagerness betrays you,

Your casualness the key,

I'm very much aware,

That you are always watching me.

I've fantasized about you,
Though you would never know.
And I pretend I do not care,
When you say you must go.
I hide my thoughts within me,
I try to stem their flow,
I try to calm my pounding heart,
And hope it doesn't show.

If we could plan the moment,
If we could course a chart,
If you were free, and I could gladly
Offer you my heart.
Would we belong together?
And wish to never part?
Or would we want this over,
Wishing we'd not let it start?

I must just go on dreaming,

Fantasizing of the day,

You sweep me in your arms,

And kiss my loneliness away.

I'll daydream about tenderness,

And all the things you'd say,

And in my world of make believe,

You'd be mine come what may.

Ah here you are again,

Pretending not to care at all.

Watching every move I make,

And longing for the call.

Burning just as I am,

Safely hid behind that wall.

Scared to make a move in case,

Instead you take a fall.

We'll never know the answer,
You will never feel my touch.
You'll never lean on me,
For I shall never be your crutch.
We shall not speak of love,
We shall not ever mean that much,
Imagining what cannot be,
Each sweet caress and such.

You think I do not know
That you want me as I do you.
You think I go about my day,
And do not have a clue.
I wonder what would happen,
I wonder what you'd do,
If you found out that all along,
Yes all along I knew.

The Last Goodbye

I watch your face as sunlight
Filters through the window pane.
I see your eyelids flutter
As you dream of us again.

Those lines upon your face
Hold all the memories we share.
Each gentle fold and crease remind me
Just how much I care.

I've loved you for so many years,

I think you know how much.

A love like this goes deeper,

Far beyond the human touch.

We've had some good times haven't we?

We've laughed until we cried.

We've had our share of sorrows too,

And all our friends have died.

I wonder where the years went?

How could time have gone so fast?

How could a lifetime disappear?

How can I be the last?

They say that youth is wasted
On the young, I know that's true.
There's so much more I want to say,
There's so much more to do.

But these old bones won't take me,
I don't care to go alone.
I'll just sit here and reminisce
On all the life we've known.

Your gentle face, still sleeping,
Still unaware I'm here,
That face I've loved for all these years,
Sees not this falling tear.

I'm so glad that I know you.

You are everything and more.

We have made a life worth living.

We have opened every door.

I listen to your breathing,

Hold your hand to let you know,

You do not have to stay for me,

I'm here so you can go.

And so it's time to say Goodbye,

It's time for you to leave.

It's time for you to feel no pain,

It's time for me to grieve.

The evening shadows come, like you
The daylight starts to fade.
The time for leaving rushes
Past the memories we've made.

This last Goodbye between us,
Is the parting of our ways.
Don't wait for me; I'll join you soon,
We'll then know endless days.

Best Friends

When they said there was something wrong

I didn't want to know.

I tried to block out all their words,

And not let feelings show.

Aware that you were watching me

I forced myself to smile.

Hoping I could fool you and

Pretend a little while.

I gently held you in my arms,

And softly said your name.

I gazed into your deep brown eyes

And saw they held no blame.

We've been together many years,

I cannot let you leave,

My mind was reeling from such thoughts

When you tugged at my sleeve.

You've always been there for me,

You have loved me from day one,

And I don't want to think of life

Alone when you have gone.

You are a loyal companion,
I could never ask for more.
You love me even now I know,
And offer me your paw.

Your tail is gently wagging,
Even now you understand.
You know that I will let you go
And thus you lick my hand.

I'll stay until it's over,
I'll let you go in peace.
My dearest friend I'll wait with you,
I'll stay until you cease.

My photographs show memories,

Of a journey we both shared.

When love was given freely

We both knew the other cared.

One day I'll find another,

Someone else to take your place.

But I shall not forget you nor

Shall I forget your face.

The Fifth Day

We were leaving that old country,

For a new one shining bright.

We were leaving all we'd ever known,

And giving up the fight.

We hoped to start a new life,

Thought the course we'd set was true.

We took our children with us,

Like good parents were meant to.

I remember we kept laughing,

So excited to be free.

Living our adventure,

As we all set out to sea.

The days passed like a dream,

And dreams were filled with joy and hope.

On waking I remember thinking,

This time we will cope.

But none of this was meant to be.

No future called our name.

With no clue what was coming,

We all ran towards the flame.

One night whilst we were sleeping,

We were woken by a fear.

It seemed we'd hit an iceberg,

And no rescue ships were near.

Alone at sea and frantic,

With no one we could depend.

My husband looked at me,

We both knew this would be the end.

We went back to our cabin.

There was nothing else to do.

Trapped below in steerage,

Caught in a fate we knew.

I couldn't stop from shaking,
So I held my children tight.
Aware too much of what would come,
That awful fateful night.

I gave my children whiskey,
Sang them to a drunken sleep.
Hoping they would not know when
The Reaper came to reap.

And thus we lay together,
Holding hands we prayed our last.
With no hope for a future,
Clinging uselessly to past.

When rescue came we knew not.

We were not to see the dawn.

Trapped within that icy place

With no one left to mourn.

A shattered dream left broken.

Four lives not meant to live.

Tricked by fate so cruelly,

Taking all we had to give.

In icy waters waiting,

Had we known that we would delve,

We never would have board that ship,

In April Nineteen Twelve.

The Angel

I watched an angel walking,

Through the gently falling snow,

Surprised at first to see her,

She was unaware I know.

I saw she left no footprint,

Nor trace from either wing,

And watching her I felt my heart,

As it began to sing.

She walked with such clear clarity,
She walked with gentle poise,
And I could tell from where I sat,
That she made not a noise.
I watched her with a bated breath,
I watched with awed delight,
Amazed at that before me,
Inspired by such a sight.

The moon cast silver shadows,
I could see her clear as day,
I reached as though to touch,
But knew I couldn't make her stay.
The snow kept falling as it
Deeply blanketed the ground,
Cleansing all it fell upon,
And quieting all sound.

This moment, oh this moment,

I will carry evermore,

That winters night when sleep escaped,

And I saw what I saw.

That unassuming angel,

I did not expect to find,

Who touched my heart so deeply,

And never leaves my mind.

Watching quietly from my shadows,

Comforted that lonely night,

As slowly she began to fade,

And disappear from sight.

Then just before I lost her,

She turned smiling with such grace,

It dawned on me, that all along,

She'd known my hiding place.

From there on every Christmas Eve,

When all else are asleep,

I wait, sat by that window,

In the darkness of the deep.

I wait in hope she finds me,

Our paths to cross again,

Although inside I know

That this desire is all in vain.

They say hope springs eternal,

It has overflowed my soul,

It has kept me warm on bitter nights,

And helped to keep me whole.

The vision I cannot forget,

That piece of her I share,

When silent words upon my lips,

Became a whispered prayer.

Years pass by and children grow,

And yet I will remain,

With Christmas magic in my heart,

And so much love to gain.

Remembering an evening,

When nothing stirred but me,

And angels walked among us,

With only I to see.

April

I thought I'd take this moment
To write and let you know,
You mean the very world to me,
Though sometimes I don't show.

I wish I could take time back,
Wish I could hold you now.
I meant those promises I made,
I meant each word and vow.

I don't have much to tell you.
There isn't much to say.
I've never been too good with words,
They just get in the way.

I could not face this nightmare
Without you in my heart.
I've seen so many awful things,
I don't know where to start.

If this has taught me one thing,
It's love must hold the key.
Though love seems far away right now,
So very far from me.

But if I close my eyes I
Can see you standing there.
It helps to know you wait for me,
And know how much you care.

I love you even more now,
I hope you know how much.
I cannot wait to hold you close,
Or feel your loving touch.

I know it's spring where you are,
And flowers bloom galore.
I see you walking in those fields,
As I walk fields of War.

This silence is so precious,

Though I know it cannot last.

They say we're on the move again,

And soon the bombs will blast.

I must go now my darling,

I hope I'll be home soon.

There's talk that maybe we could be

Back home again by June.

I've had my fill of fighting,

I pray that this will end.

I hope you feel the love within

This letter that I send.

Journeys End

One eve when I alone in bed,

Eluded dreams to fill my head,

Succumbed to fate that sleepless night,

And rose to wait the mornings light.

A lonely candle as my friend,

For company until nights end.

The only noise,- a ticking clock,

On and on tick- tock, tick- tock.

When I at last could take no more,
I dressed, and ventured past the door.
The moon was full, and lit my way,
I knew not where, (or so I say).

I walked the path, went through the gate,
My feet were fast, they would not wait.
Past the houses dark and still,
Through the village, up the hill.

Up and on where land meets sea,
With gentle winds caressing me.
Why the hurry? Why such haste?
I felt there was no time to waste.

I turned at last to breathe the view,

Unleash my mind, and think of you.

But thoughts of you would run from mind,

For there was someone else to find.

I saw her in the moonlights glare.

Standing, silent, unaware.

She searched the ocean from up high,

That lonely silhouette on sky.

I noticed she wore clothes of old,

And, unaffected by the cold,

She merely stood in vacant stare,

And watched the sea, just standing there.

She did not move, she did not breathe,
I did not even see her leave.
A blink, that's all, and she was gone,
And I was left the only one.

I walked towards that cliff top edge.
I peeked below that dangerous ledge.
But she was gone, fled from this coast,
That lonely figure, now a ghost.

Much like a ghost myself I stood.
I scanned the sky, it did no good.
I thought of you out in that night,
And wondered were you far in flight?

Risking all that we stay free,

Has kept you, oh so far from me.

My aching heart has longed to know

That once returned, you will not go.

A heart entwined is never free.

When parted it weeps silently.

Just like that woman I shall wait,

No matter how the hour is late.

I think of all the lovers past,

Who long for loves embrace at last.

Of all the women through the years,

Who've stood right here, and fought back tears.

How many ghosts have felt as I?
Searching the land, the sea, the sky.
A precious hope that all is well,
And you are unharmed in that hell.

A life on hold, my life in fear.
I want my arms to feel you here.
This waiting fills my heart with pain
And dread, to not see you again.

My love I wait, and pray you will,
Return to me, and love me still.
So, like that ghost, I will not bend,
'Til you be here at journeys end.

CPSIA information can be obtained
at www.ICGtesting.com
Printed in the USA
LVOW04s0509301215
468235LV00005B/6/P